DECORATING
denim

DECORATING
denim

designer glitz for
denim, includes **35**
step-by-step projects

ALISON SPANYOL

CICO BOOKS
LONDON NEW YORK

First published in 2007 by CICO Books
an imprint of Ryland Peters & Small
519 Broadway, 5th Floor, New York, NY 10012

10 9 8 7 6 5 4 3 2 1

A CIP catalog record for this book is available from the Library of Congress

ISBN-13: 978 1 904991 91 5
ISBN-10: 1 904991 91 2

Printed in China

Editor: Sarah Hoggett
Designer: Janet James
Photographer: Tino Tedaldi
Illustrators: Kate Simunek (step-by-step projects) and
Stephen Dew (techniques section and templates)

CONTENTS

INTRODUCTION

Denim is the one thing that everyone has in his or her wardrobe —
and that means that it can sometimes be difficult to create a look
that's really individual. Or maybe you have a favorite pair of jeans
that's looking a little tired or even completely worn out. Rather than
throw them out, why not give them a new lease on life by applying
some of the ideas in this book?

You don't have to spend a fortune to personalize a garment and
make it look great. You will probably already have a lot of things
that you can use — off-cuts, remnants, buttons, and sequins from
other craft projects, for example. You can also recycle old clothes:
an old patterned shirt or top can provide a surprising amount of
material, and the buttons, poppers, hooks, and eyes can all be
useful. Other things that you might need are available from craft
shops but if they haven't got what you are looking for, try thrift
stores, garage sales, and markets for everything from inspiring
vintage fabrics to bright trims. Many of these projects combine
denim with materials that one might not expect. Silks, satins, lace,
and velvet create a contrast and can give a utilitarian garment a
really feminine touch.

The projects in this book represent a wide range of possibilities,
from the simple to the elaborate, from the subtle to the
outlandishly colorful, from the elegant to the light-hearted. Don't
worry if you're not a skilled seamstress — you don't have to be. If
you are not familiar with some of the techniques or stitches, the
easy-to-follow step-by-step diagrams will make everything clear.

Of course, you don't have to follow the instructions to the letter.
You will probably have ideas and variations of your own and you
may well come up with projects completely different to anything in
this book. I have by no means exhausted all the possibilities of
decorating denim and I hope that you will see this book as a
starting point for future decorative projects. You may sometimes
need a little patience, but I hope that what you see will enthuse
and inspire you.

Jeans are the most popular of all denim garments, and it's a safe bet that most of us have several pairs tucked away in our wardrobes! With so many mass-produced jeans available, it can sometimes be hard to stand out from the crowd — but this chapter contains a wealth of design ideas to inspire you, from simple sequins and buttons to delicate embroidery.

jeans

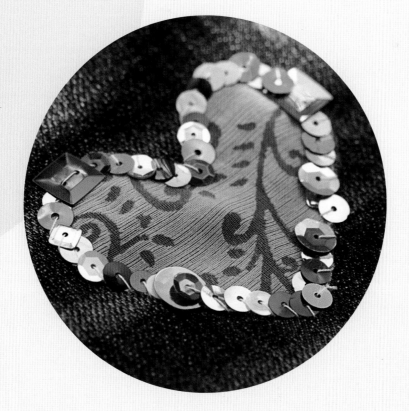

BABY FACE jeans

Embellished with a tassel trim and sparkling sequins, these jeans bring to mind visions of showgirls and the circus. Of course, you could change the words to something more personal — a nickname or a private joke, perhaps. Whatever you choose, keep the hand-written quality of the lettering. It's your name that's up in lights (well, in sequins, at least!).

you will need

Template on page 126
Tracing paper and pencil
Tailor's chalk or fabric marker pen
Scrap of pink blanket material
Iron-on diamanté studs
Silver sequins
Deep pink velvet ribbon
Green tasselled upholstery trim
Flowered and sequinned material
Needle and sewing thread

1. Enlarge the template on page 126 to the required size and transfer the words onto pink blanket material (see page 119). Cut out.

2. Stitch silver sequins onto the words (see page 125), and then slipstitch the words onto the back pockets (see page 121). Add iron-on diamanté studs to the loops of the letters "y" and "f", and position a few studs randomly over the pockets.

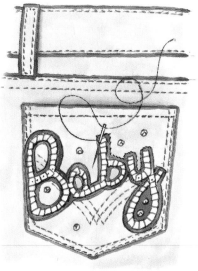

3. Slipstitch a strip of deep pink velvet ribbon to the top of each pocket, and then stitch a strip of green, tasselled upholstery trim above that, with the bottom of the tassels level with the bottom of the ribbon.

4. Cut out three flowers from the sequinned material. (If you can't find a similar flowery sequinned material, draw a flower shape on green organza and outline the petals in chain stitch, then attach a spiral of green sequins in the centre and individual sequins to the petal tips.) Place one flower on the right front pocket, one on the left leg below the pocket, and one on the right leg seam, and slipstitch them in place.

VINTAGE FLORAL
jeans

Vintage embroidered tablecloth
   or placemat
Pencil or fabric marker pen
Needle and embroidery threads
Assorted buttons

When you find the perfect pair of jeans, they can become the most important item in your wardrobe. This project helps you turn your trusted, favorite jeans into a unique and contemporary fashion piece. I love vintage embroidery, hand stitched with such care by someone in the past. Here, the leaves and blossom curl around the leg and hip, creating a pretty and delicate effect. A variety of buttons on the pocket and hip add texture and interest.

1. Select the sections of embroidery that you want to use on your jeans and draw around them with a pencil or fabric marker.

2. Using embroidery thread in a toning color, chain stitch along your drawn line (see page 123). Carefully cut out the motifs, cutting as close as possible to the stitching.

3. Pin the pieces in place. Stitch them in place by working blanket stitch (see page 123) through the links of the chain stitch. Sew a few buttons to the tops of the pockets and the legs to complete.

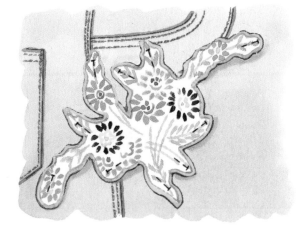

IT'S ALL IN THE DETAIL

LAZY DAISY
jeans

I just love the big daisies on these jeans. A piece of trim such as this is so useful, as it gives you a starting point for a design and you need only a small piece to create a great effect. The soft green silk, blue lace, and twinkling pearls and sequins give the background to the daisy on the turn-up a watery look, while another one sways above it in the breeze on a delicately embroidered stem.

you will need

Green silk fabric
Blue lace trim
Daisy-motif fabric trim
Gold sequins
Pearl beads
Sewing needle
Thread to match the lace
White embroidery thread

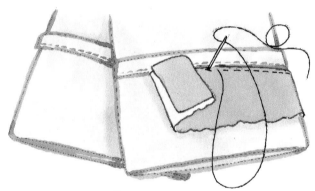

1. Turn up the bottom hem of the jeans to the outside and stitch in place at the side seams. Measure the circumference of each leg at the base, and cut a strip of green silk fabric to this length and about two-thirds the depth of the turn-up. Leaving the edges raw, stitch the silk to the turn-up, just under the hem, using running stitch (see page 120).

2. Cut out pieces of blue lace trim, and pin them to the turn-ups. Using running stitch and sewing thread to match the lace, stitch the lace trim in place, stitching through both the silk and the denim.

IT'S ALL IN THE DETAIL

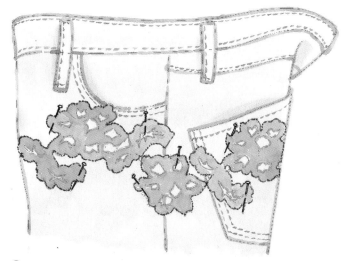

3. Pin, and then stitch more pieces of blue lace trim over the left front pocket, the side seam, and the back pocket.

4. Cut out three daisies from the fabric trim. Stitch one to the center of a lace flower on the front of each turn-up, and one to the right leg about 6 in. (15 cm) above the top of the turn-up.

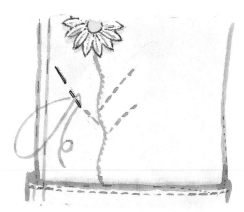

5. Using white embroidery thread, work a wavy line of chain stitch (see page 123) from the center of the daisy on the right leg to just below the top of the turn-up. Work three small stems in running stitch, coming off the main stem at an angle of about 45˚.

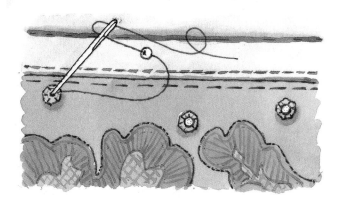

6. Sew a gold sequin, with a tiny pearl bead in the center, to the end of each side stem (see page 125).

7. Sew more sequins and pearl beads randomly over the green silk on the turn-ups.

The use of silk and lace gives this design a luxurious, ultra-feminine feel, while the tiny sequins and pearl beads scattered randomly over the fabric add a sexy shimmer. Although it looks sophisticated, only minimal sewing skills are required.

PATCHWORK HEART
jeans

The most important thing in making this design work is your choice of fabrics, so make sure you choose fabrics that complement each other. I used fabrics featuring old roses, candy-colored stripes, blue denim, and heart shapes which, when combined, are reminiscent of traditional, country-style patchwork.

you will need

Scraps of blue denim, floral, and striped fabrics
Embroidery threads in contrasting colors
Fabric scissors
Sewing machine
Contrasting sewing thread

1. Cut four different-sized rectangles of floral and striped fabric. Pin them to the right leg of your jeans, as shown; the left-hand edges should align, with one piece overhanging the right-hand edge a little, to provide a more interesting shape. Machine stitch the pieces in place. (Alternatively, hand stitch them using backstitch.)

2. Cut a small rectangle of old denim and fray the edges to a depth of about ¼ in. (0.5 cm). Fold it in half, and cut out a heart shape.

3. Place the piece on a floral section of the patchwork, so that the pattern can be seen through the cut-out shape. Using tiny running stitches (see page 120), stitch it in place using a contrasting color of embroidery thread. Stitch around the edge of the cut-out shape, too, to prevent it from fraying.

4. Cut a large rectangle of denim fabric and fray the edges to a depth of about ¼ in. (0.5 cm). Pin it over the patchwork section and the seam, so that it wraps around the leg. Backstitch it in place (see page 121), and then work a row of cross stitch (see page 124) around the edge, on top of the machine stitching.

5. Apply other patches to the front left leg, as shown, and work a wavy line of chain stitch (see page 123) along one edge of one patch.

6. Cut one piece of denim roughly the same size as the back pockets, fold it in half, and cut out a heart shape, as in Step 2. Place a piece of floral fabric behind the cut-out shape. Using tiny stitches, backstitch the cut-out heart shape to one pocket and the denim-and-floral patch to the other, making sure that you do not stitch the pockets closed.

FALLING LEAVES
jeans

This design is all about the weather — fall leaves blowing about, drops of silvery rain, and even a hint of frost with those cool blue leaves. Your eye is drawn down to the bottom of the legs, where the leaves and rain are gently drifting. The wavy lines of sequins help to suggest this movement.

you will need

Imitation rose leaves
Shiny, glittery blue fabric
Blue glitter dimensional fabric paint
Square silver sequins
Needle
Orange and white sewing threads
Orange embroidery thread

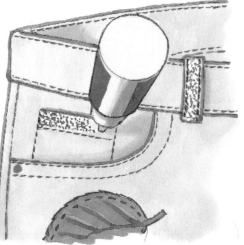

1. Using running stitch (see page 120) and orange sewing thread, sew imitation rose leaves under both front pockets and to the lower right leg of the jeans in a trailing pattern. Add a couple of leaves to the left leg, too. Cut three or four leaves from shiny, glittery blue fabric and attach them to the jeans in the same way.

2. Using blue glitter dimensional fabric paint, "draw" around the edges of the blue leaves; this will help prevent the fabric from fraying. Draw over some of the veins of the rose leaves with the glitter paint, and apply a line of paint to the edge of the pockets.

3. Using orange embroidery thread, work a wavy line of chain stitch (see page 123) through the center of the blue fabric leaves.

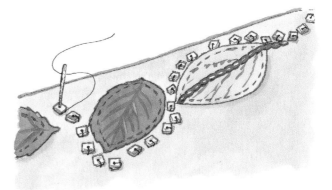

4. Using white thread, attach square silver sequins in a wavy line, running through the cascade of falling leaves (see page 125).

FLOWER AND IVY
jeans

The denim flower was the starting point for this design, but then it just grew and grew! I took my inspiration for the trailing ivy leaves from the border on a Victorian print, and added a bit of glittery fabric paint to give them a fresh, frosty feel. Using dimensional fabric paint is a fun and effective way to decorate jeans. It's also very quick to do — although you do need to allow plenty of time for the paint to dry thoroughly.

you will need

Old blue denim including a back
   pocket
Lace
Pale blue leather ribbon
5 small velvet flowers
1 pearl button
4 star-shaped sequins
4 glass beads
1 strip of diamanté
Sequin fabric
Fabric marker pen or tailor's chalk
Dimensional fabric paints: blue
   glitter, white, pink
Selection of thin ribbons in
   shades of blue, lilac, and silver

1. Cut four flower shapes in different sizes — three from old denim and one from lace, with the lace flower being the second smallest. Apply dots of blue glitter dimensional fabric paint to the denim flowers.

2. Layer the flowers together on the left leg of the jeans, just below the pocket, according to their size. Lay two lengths of pale blue leather ribbon across the flower in a cross shape, then place a velvet flower in the middle, with a pearl button at its center. Stitching through the button and all layers of fabric, stitch the flowers to the jeans. Make sure you catch the ribbons, too.

IT'S ALL IN THE DETAIL

3. Using neat running stitch (see page 120), stitch around the outside edges of the flower petals to attach them firmly to the jeans.

4. Position the remaining four velvet flowers on the left leg of the jeans, with a star-shaped sequin in the center of each one and a glass bead in the center of each sequin, and stitch in place.

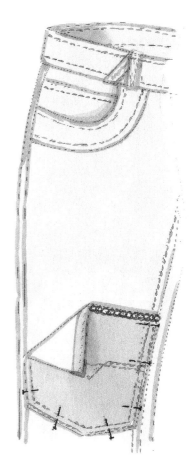

5. Cut the back pocket off an old pair of jeans. Sew a diamanté strip across the top of the pocket. Using matching thread, slipstitch the pocket to the right leg of the jeans (see page 121), around the mid-thigh point, leaving the top edge open.

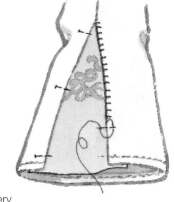

The trailing stems of ivy in this design are simple to draw freehand. I decorated the leaves with fabric paint to contrast with the bold 3-D flowers, but you could embroider them instead, using chain or backstitch for the outlines and satin stitch to fill in the leaf centers.

6. Using a fabric marker pen or tailor's chalk, draw a trailing ivy-leaf design freehand down both legs of the jeans. Outline the leaves in white dimensional fabric paint and the stems in pink. Fill in the centers of the leaves with blue glitter dimensional fabric paint.

7. Unpick the outer seam of each leg from the hemline up to the mid-calf point. Cut a triangle of sequinned fabric and pin it behind the opened-out section. Using white embroidery thread, blanket stitch (see page 123) the sequinned fabric to the side seams. Turn the jeans wrong side out and slipstitch the edges of the sequinned fabric to the jeans, to hold them secure.

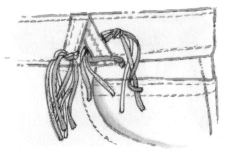

8. For each belt loop, cut three 10-in. (25-cm) lengths of different ribbons and tie in a knot in the center. Then tie one ribbon bundle to each belt loop to create a tassel.

SEQUINNED HEARTS
jeans

These jeans have a fun, carefree look and make me think of being young. The repeated heart motif is like a doodle, the kind of thing you used to draw over and over on your pencil case or school books. There is also the hint of disco glitter around the highlighted little pocket, perfect for your lip gloss!

you will need

Tailor's chalk
Silver sequin fabric
Gold sequins
Pearl buttons
Embroidery threads
Patterned fabric
Colored sequins
Silver glitter dimensional fabric
  paint
Needle
Sewing threads

1. Using a fabric marker pen or tailor's chalk, draw four hearts on the jeans — two small ones on the top of the right leg, one small one at the top of the left leg, and a larger one at the bottom of the right leg. Using small, sharp scissors, carefully cut out the center of the three small hearts.

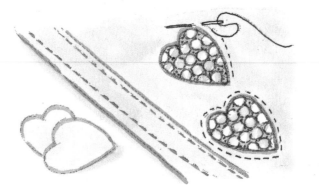

2. Place a small piece of silver sequinned fabric behind each of the two cut-out hearts on the right leg and stitch in place by hand, by working a single line of running stitch (see page 120) in a contrasting color of thread about ¼ in. (0.5 cm) beyond the edge of each hole.

IT'S ALL IN THE DETAIL

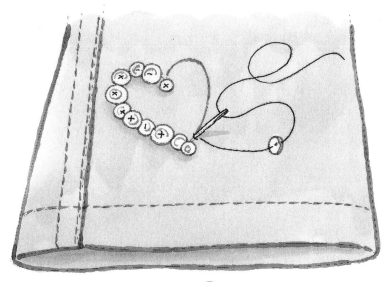

3. Stitch pearl buttons in different sizes around the heart at the bottom of the right leg.

4. Cut two small hearts from patterned fabric. Using running stitch, attach one below the pocket on the left leg, and then sew colored sequins in varying sizes around the edge (see page 125).

5. Place a square of patterned fabric behind the cut-out heart shape on the left leg, and pin in place. Work a line of chain stitch (see page 123) in a contrasting color of thread about 1/4 in. (0.5 cm) beyond the edge of the hole. Overlap the second patterned heart on the cut-out heart, as shown, and stitch in place using running stitch.

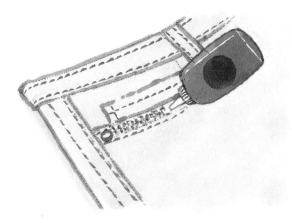

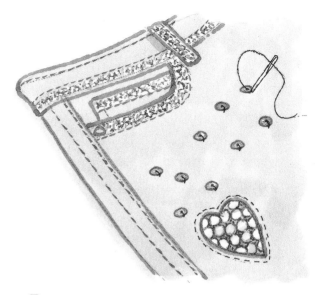

6. Apply silver glitter dimensional fabric paint along the top of the pockets, the bottom edge of the waistband, and the belt loops.

7. Stitch gold sequins randomly over the top of the right leg, above the hearts.

PAISLEY
jeans

I really love paisley: it's such a pleasing shape. I love the flow and movement between the different elements. These pieces were cut from a silk tie, and it's as if I have set them free to swirl and bounce about on the jeans. The gold outlines help to heighten this effect.

1. Using small, sharp scissors, cut out paisley shapes from your chosen fabric. Place them on scrap paper, draw around the edge of each shape with gold glitter dimensional fabric paint, and leave to dry.

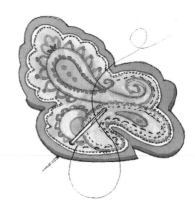

2. Place some of the paisley shapes on PVC or satin fabric. Carefully cut around each shape, leaving a narrow border all around. (Other pieces are left without a fabric backing.)

3. Using running stitch (see page 120) and matching thread, stitch the paisley pieces to the background fabrics. (You can use a sewing machine to do this if you prefer.)

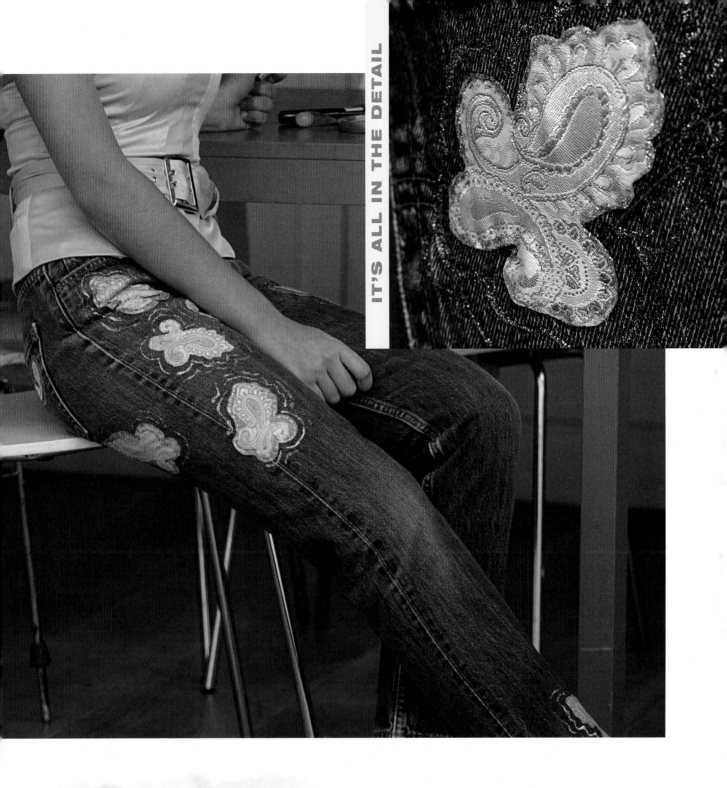

4. Place the pieces on your jeans, leaving space between them. When you're happy with the arrangement, slipstitch them in place (see page 121). Draw around the outside of each shape with gold and silver glitter dimensional fabric paint, and leave to dry.

paisley jeans ✳ **33**

BRODERIE ANGLAISE
jeans

The broderie anglaise trim, practical side pockets, and simple, stenciled motifs give these jeans a rustic feel. I highlighted some areas of the stencils with glitter and sequins but deliberately left other parts looking slightly faded, in keeping with the pale, washed denim, as I feel it's important for the decoration to be in a style that's sympathetic to the original item.

Broderie anglaise tablecloth
Pearl fabric paint
Small paintbrush
Old dark blue denim jeans
Broderie anglaise trim
Blue glitter dimensional fabric
   paint
Sequins
Sewing machine
Sewing thread
Needle
White embroidery thread

1. Place a broderie anglaise tablecloth on the jeans to use as a stencil and, using pearl fabric paint and a small paintbrush, apply paint through the holes to transfer the pattern to the fabric. Leave to dry.

IT'S ALL IN THE DETAIL

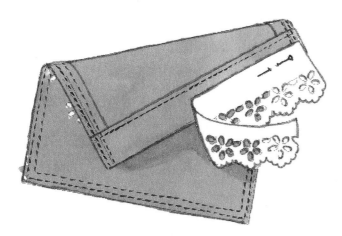

2. Cut the bottom part of one leg off an old pair of dark blue denim jeans, and unpick the side seams to give two pieces. Using a sewing machine, hem all raw edges of both pieces. Stencil a motif on each piece, as in Step 1, and leave to dry. Sew a strip of broderie anglaise trim across the top of each piece.

3. Slipstitch (see page 121) the two pieces to your jeans around the mid-thigh point, over the outer seam of each leg, leaving the top edge open to form a pocket.

4. Stencil two more motifs onto dark blue denim. Using blue glitter dimensional fabric paint, join up the leaves on the motifs to form a stem. Form stems on the stenciled pattern on the jeans in the same way. Leave to dry.

5. Sew sequins to the center of the stenciled flowers (see page 125), applying a single sequin to some flowers and a small circle of sequins to others.

Blue and white is a classic and perennially popular color combination. Here, I've used patches of dark blue denim to contrast with the mid-blue of the jeans and add drama to an otherwise simply executed design.

6. Cut a pocket shape from one of the motifs that you stencilled in Step 4 and a random, abstract shape from the other. Using blanket stitch (see page 123) and white embroidery thread, attach these pieces to the right front leg, as shown.

DAISY FLOWER EMBROIDERED
jeans

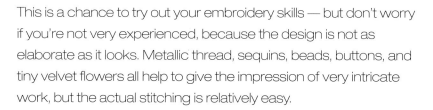

This is a chance to try out your embroidery skills — but don't worry if you're not very experienced, because the design is not as elaborate as it looks. Metallic thread, sequins, beads, buttons, and tiny velvet flowers all help to give the impression of very intricate work, but the actual stitching is relatively easy.

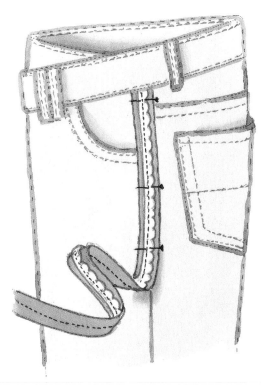

1. Cut two lengths of blue satin ribbon and two lengths of lace the same length as the legs of your jeans, from the waistband to the hem. Machine stitch one piece of lace down the center of each ribbon. Turn under the short ends. Using thread to match the ribbon, slipstitch one piece over each outer leg seam by hand (see page 121).

IT'S ALL IN THE DETAIL

2. Working freehand and using a marker pen or tailor's chalk, draw a flowing flower and leaf pattern on the legs of the jeans, with a large, daisy-type flower on the right leg. Using white embroidery thread, embroider the daisy in stem stitch (see page 122). Stitch a small pearl button in the center of the flower.

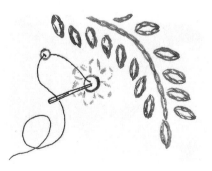

3. Now embroider the remaining flowers. Use running stitch (see page 120) for the small flowers, and chain stitch (see page 123) for the stems and leaves. I used metallic blue thread for the trailing stems at the top and bottom of the large daisy to add a slight shimmer, but you could use white thread throughout if you prefer.

4. Embellish the small running-stitch flowers by stitching a sequin topped by a tiny bead to the center of two of the flowers, and a sequin only to the others (see page 125). Add a glass flower button.

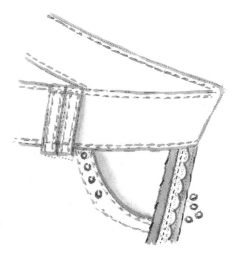

5. Position two flower-shaped sequins randomly on the embroidery and stitch them in place, with a small pink or purple glass bead in the center for extra sparkle.

6. Following the manufacturer's instructions, apply tiny self-adhesive gemstones around the tops of the pockets.

Buttons make really
effective flower centers,
in a fraction of the time
that it would take to
embroider such details,
while sequins and beads
provide a sparkle and
contrast in texture that
can really "lift" a design.

BLUE ROSE
jeans

The traditional blue roses and pretty gold leaves remind me of English decorated porcelain. Here, I have given the motif a thoroughly modern twist through the choice of materials: the gold leather leaves are crisp and stylish and, combined with the square silver sequins, give the design sharpness and a contemporary edge.

- Flowered fabric
- Blue pearl sequins
- Scraps of gold leather
- Silver sequins
- Needle
- Embroidery threads in matching colors
- Small, sharp scissors

1. Select three flowers from your chosen fabric — two large and one small. Using matching thread, chain stitch around each one (see page 123), and then cut out, cutting as close to the stitching as possible.

2. Stitch one large flower to each back pocket by working blanket stitch (see page 123) through the loops of the chain stitch outline. Make sure that you only stitch through the top layer of fabric, so that you do not stitch the pockets closed.

IT'S ALL IN THE DETAIL

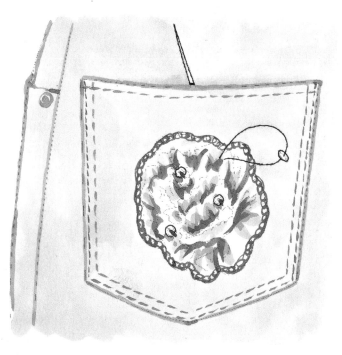

3. Stitch tiny blue pearl sequins randomly over the flowers (see page 125). Again, make sure that you do not stitch the pockets closed.

4. Cut leaf shapes from gold leather. Sew them in place, using tiny running stitches (see page 120) and blue thread to match the flowers.

5. Sew tendrils of silver sequins across the center of the back pockets (see page 125), extending outward from the flowers, with another row of sequins across the tops of the pockets.

6. Apply the small flower and three small gold leaves to the right front leg, as in Steps 2 and 4.

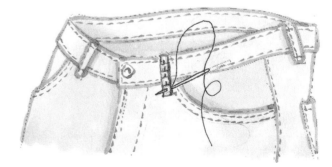

7. Sew silver sequins over the front belt loops.

'60s RIVIERA
jeans

Patterned silk headscarf

Dimensional fabric paint to
    match the background color
    of the headscarf

Swirly-patterned pink fabric

Gold fabric

Bright pink flowery fabric

Scraps of pink, orange, and
    purple woollen fabric or felt

Iron-on diamanté studs

Pink lace trim

Pale pink sequins

Tiny pearl beads

Yellow floral trim

Needle

Embroidery threads

These jeans are definitely for summer holidays in hot sunshine.
They make me think of St Tropez and the French Riviera in the
1960s — perhaps because of the '60s-inspired swirly design on the
pink silk fabric. These jeans are show-off pieces and there's a lot
going on — layering, clashing, and mixing of textures and colors.
Cheerful and attention seeking, they just make me smile!

1. Using dimensional fabric paint, draw a line around the
printed design on the headscarf. Leave to dry. Cut out,
cutting as close as possible to the painted line. The paint
prevents the edge of the silk from fraying.

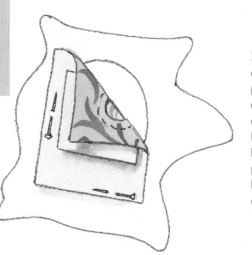

2. Cut an oval shape out of the
center of the main motif. Take a
piece of swirly-patterned fabric large
enough to fit behind the oval, and
cut a heart shape out of the center.
Place gold fabric behind the cut-out
heart, and work running stitch (see
page 120) around the edge of the
heart. Pin the swirly fabric behind the
oval and blanket stitch (see page
123) around the edge.

3. Cut four small flower motifs from bright pink flowery fabric. Using running stitch and matching thread, sew them onto the swirly-patterned oval. Pin and baste the whole motif to the left front leg of the jeans, below the pocket, then blanket stitch in place, using thread in a toning color.

4. Cut small leaf shapes from woollen fabric or felt. Following the manufacturer's instructions, apply iron-on diamantés to some of them. Arrange them on the left front leg of the jeans and stitch in place, using running stitch and matching thread.

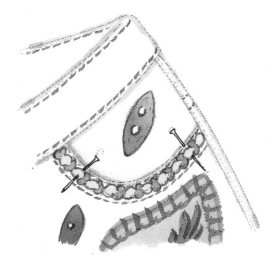

5. Cut pieces of pink lace trim. Using running stitch, sew one piece below the front right pocket and up over the waistband and one to the bottom of the left front leg. Decorate the lace with pale pink sequins and tiny pearl beads, as shown.

6. Sew a piece of yellow floral trim to the base of the left front pocket.

7. Repeat Steps 1–3 to make a smaller motif for the right front leg, reserving the cut-out heart shape from the center. Blanket stitch this motif to the bottom of the right front leg and the cut-out heart shape to the right turn-up.

Thrift stores and garage sales can be a good source of vintage scarves and, if you plan your design carefully and reserve any cut-out sections for use in other projects, you can make a small piece of fabric go a long way. Another useful tip is to replicate motifs from your vintage scarf in a less expensive fabric, such as felt.

FLAG jeans

Each of the two flags on these jeans is an iconic symbol — yet its elements can be distilled down to very basic shapes that are still clearly recognizable. For me, one of the keys to the design is to make the edges of the flags wavy to suggest the movement of flags blowing in the breeze.

1. Put an old book or a magazine inside the legs of the jeans and, keeping the fabric taut, scrape a Stanley knife backward and forward across the fabric to distress and age it.

2. Cut two small rectangles of light blue denim, to use as the base for the two flags. For the Union Jack flag, cut a cross and four strips of medium-blue denim fabric. Baste and then machine stitch them in place on one base rectangle. Cut eight triangles of dark blue denim, and baste and then machine stitch them in place. Machine stitch all around the edges of the flag, and then slipstitch it onto the front right leg of the jeans, a little way above the knee (see page 121).

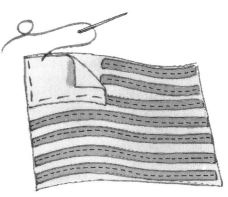

3. To make the Stars and Stripes flag, cut four long and three short strips of dark blue denim fabric and a small rectangle of light blue denim. Pin, and then machine stitch the strips to the light blue base flag that you cut in Step 2. Stitch the small rectangle to the top left of the base flag, so that it covers the ends of the short strips. Machine stitch all around the edges of the flag, and then slipstitch it onto the left leg of the jeans, just below the pocket.

4. Using a seam ripper, remove the back right pocket of the jeans. Using tailor's chalk, draw seven stars on light blue denim fabric, and cut out. Using running stitch (see page 120), sew them onto the pocket, spacing them randomly. Sew the back pocket back onto the jeans at an angle, as shown, revealing unfaded dark blue denim beneath.

CHEF'S
special jeans

Thrift stores and garage sales are a good source of vintage fabrics that you can incorporate into new designs, even if the originals are a little faded and worn in places. This lovely fabric came from a tiny, frilly 1950s dress and a few scraps of it make the perfect decoration for a budding chef's trousers! The design is so beautifully drawn that all I have done is recreate some of the objects in the fabric as simple outlines, and worked a few basic embroidery stitches over them.

you will need

Patterned fabric with kitchen-
   utensil motifs
Tailor's chalk or fabric marker pen
Needle and sewing thread to
   match the patterned fabric
White embroidery thread

1. Cut three small patches of patterned fabric with kitchen-utensil motifs. Turn under the edges and press. Slipstitch the patches of fabric in place on the front of the jeans (see page 121).

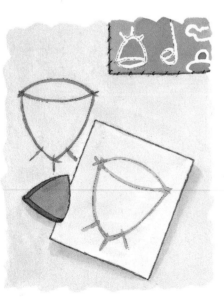

2. Enlarge the outline of some of the motifs on the fabric to the required size (see page 118) and trace them onto the jeans using tailor's chalk or a fabric marker pen (see page 119) — or draw them freehand.

3. Using white embroidery thread, chain stitch around the outlines (see page 123) and use running stitch (see page 120) for the details.

JACKSON POLLOCK
jeans

For this design, I have sewn parts of really shabby old jeans to an ordinary pair, so you get the desired worn and torn effect without having to worry about your jeans falling apart when you bend over! The paint-spattered look is inspired by the work of American abstract artist Jackson Pollock; just imagine what his jeans looked like! Just make sure you put down plenty of newspaper before you get too carried away with spattering the paint about.

you will need

Torn, old jeans
Scraps of dark denim
Fabric paint: orange, green
Paintbrush

1. Cut the front pockets off an old pair of jeans and, using tiny running stitches (see page 120), sew them below the front pockets of the jeans you are decorating. Cut one back pocket from the old jeans. Right sides together, slipstitch it (see page 121) onto the front left leg of the jeans you are decorating, below the second pocket.

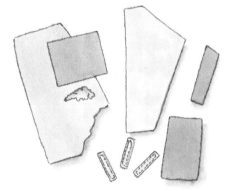

2. Cut two or three randomly shaped, torn sections out of the old jeans and a few small pieces of dark blue denim. Overlap them to form a pleasing arrangement, and stitch them to the front legs of the new jeans, using tiny running stitches. Add a few cut-off belt loops for extra decoration.

3. Cut the remaining back pocket off the old jeans. Right sides together, overlap it on the left back pocket, and overstitch it in place. Overstitch a tiny inside pocket, right side up, on top.

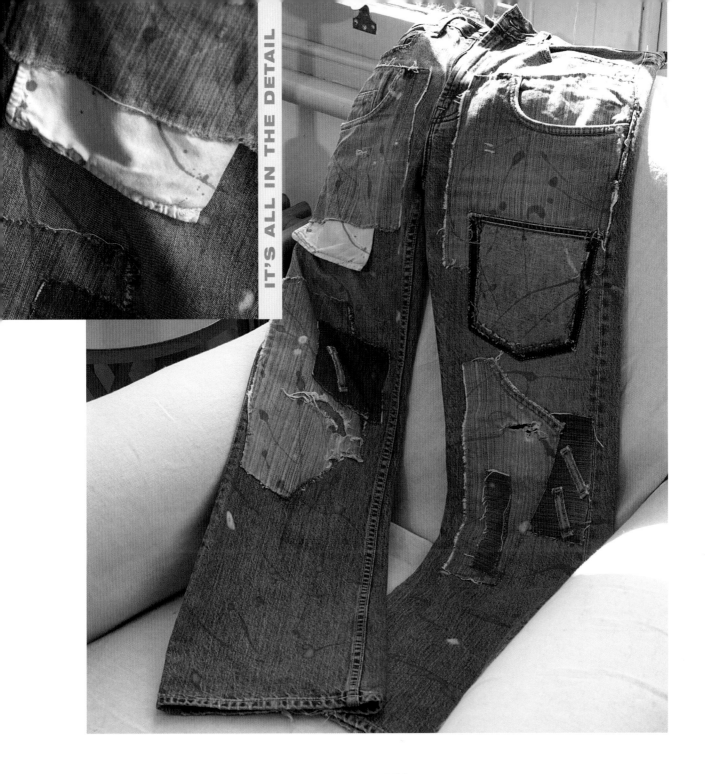

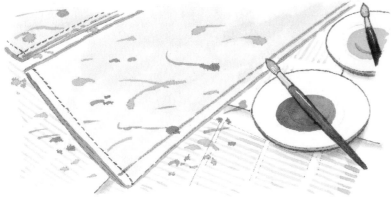

4. Put orange and green fabric paints onto old saucers or paper plates. Dip the end of a paintbrush into each color in turn, and flick the paint onto the jeans to create randomly spaced blobs and trails of color. Allow to dry thoroughly.

From contemporary casual to silky chic, this chapter showcases denim jackets to suit all kinds of occasions. Bold, bright buttons and ribbons, antique lace, and luxurious sari fabric are just a few of the decorations featured. Add a pretty little denim bag and your outfit is complete!

jackets AND bags

BUTTON
jacket

Velvet ribbon

Lots of colorful buttons

Silk ribbon printed with a floral
   pattern

Needle and matching thread

This jacket encapsulates my way of working, which is all about
collecting things and making them into something new and
different. A glass jar of buttons was my starting point, and a button
collection is something you can keep adding to. The same is true
of ribbon: if you find a ribbon you like and think it's pretty, keep it.
You'll find a use for it at some point in the future!

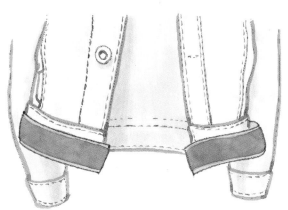

1. Measure around
the base of the jacket
and cut a length of
velvet ribbon to this
measurement, plus
about ½ in. (1 cm) to
allow for turning under
the edges.

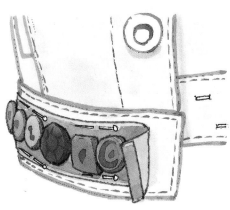

2. Sew buttons along the center of the ribbon, varying
the colors and shapes. Turn under the short ends of the
ribbon, then pin and slipstitch it to the jacket (see page
121). If there are any metal studs on the waistband, you
will need to remove them first with a pair of pliers.

3. Sew a few buttons to the left front of the jacket,
spacing them randomly. Pin and then slipstitch a piece of
floral silk ribbon across the top of the right-hand pocket,
turning under the short ends.

4. Measure the back of the jacket and cut a piece of velvet ribbon and a piece of floral silk ribbon to this length, plus about $1/2$ in. (1 cm) to allow for turning under the edges. Right sides together, machine stitch one long edge of the velvet ribbon to one long edge of the silk ribbon. Turn under the short ends, then pin and slipstitch the ribbon across the back of the jacket.

LACE PANEL
jacket

I used a very pretty piece of vintage lace as the central feature on this jacket. The lace influenced other elements of the design, such as the color of the felt and the style of the embroidery, giving the whole piece an antique feel.

you will need

- Green felt
- Lace
- Tailor's chalk or light-colored marker pen
- Scrap of gold fabric
- Needle
- Tacking thread
- Embroidery threads in colors of your choice
- Small, sharp scissors

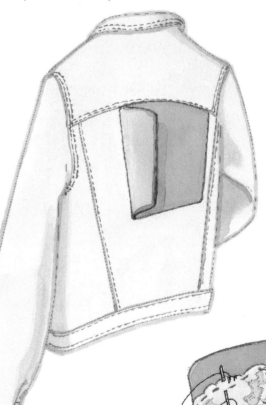

1. Measure the back panel of the jacket, and cut a piece of felt to fit it. Choose a section of lace to fit within the felt panel, and carefully cut around the edge.

2. Center the lace on top of the felt, and pin and baste it in place (see page 120). Using green embroidery thread to match the felt, blanket stitch around the edge of the lace (see page 123). Remove the basting stitches.

IT'S ALL IN THE DETAIL

3. Turn the felt over and cut away the felt behind the lace. (Use the blanket stitches as a guide to where to cut.) Repeat Steps 1–3 to make smaller, abstract-shaped felt-and-lace panels for the left sleeve and the top right front.

4. Using tailor's chalk or a light-colored marker pen, draw a swirling design and a cross on the felt panel for the back of the jacket. Using brightly colored embroidery threads, chain stitch over the outlines (see page 123). Cut a strip of felt to fit within the waistband of the center back of the jacket. Draw and chain stitch a swirling design to echo the one on the back panel.

When cutting the felt shapes for the sleeve and front of the jacket, try to echo the shapes that you have cut from the lace — but don't try to cut out every nook and cranny, or you'll end up with something that looks very fussy and fiddly.

5. Cut away the interior of the cross on the back panel. Cut a small piece of gold fabric, place it behind the chain-stitched outline, and stitch it in place by working a row of tiny running stitches horizontally and vertically over the cross (see page 120).

6. Using a contrasting color of thread, embroider two or three parallel rows of running stitch around the edges of all the swirling chain-stitched motifs.

7. Using tiny running stitches, stitch all the felt panels onto the jacket.

INSIDE-OUT
jacket

I decided to put the inside of this jacket on show, simply because the distressed appearance of the fabric made it the most interesting and pleasing side. The combination of pale and dark blues really emphasizes the collar, cuffs, and seams. I contrasted the rough denim with a rich, silky velvet and soft-patterned silk. With the addition of colorful buttons, there is no mistaking which way around it should be worn!

you will need

Tracing paper and pencil
Paper to make a pattern
Pink velvet fabric
Floral trim
Floral silk fabric
Imitation flower
Dimensional fabric paint
10 colored buttons
Sewing machine

1. Using a pair of pliers, remove all the metal studs from the jacket. Remove the pocket flaps from the front of the jacket, turn the jacket inside out, and machine stitch the flaps back in place on the inside of the jacket.

2. Trace the shape of the pocket onto paper, cut out to make a pattern, and then cut two pockets from pink velvet.

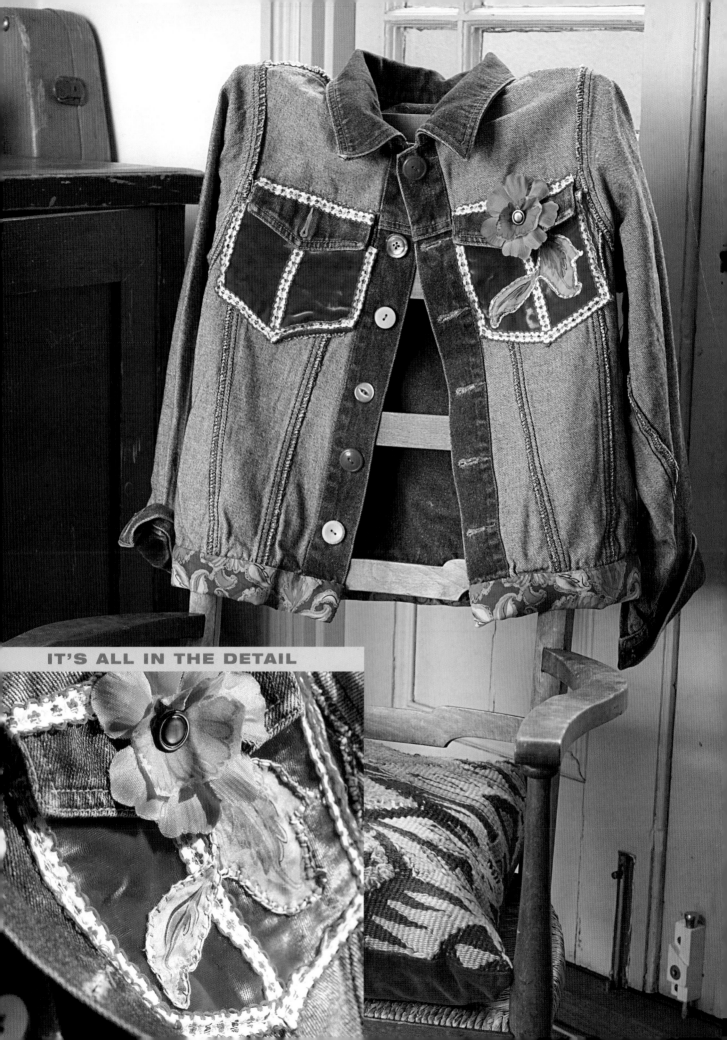

IT'S ALL IN THE DETAIL

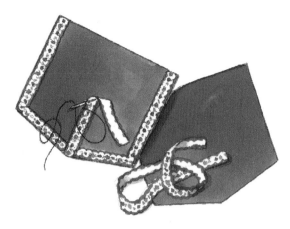

3. Edge the pockets with floral trim, stitch another length of trim vertically down the center of each pocket, and machine stitch the pockets in place. Stitch another strip of floral trim above each flap.

4. Cut a strip of floral silk fabric long enough to go all around the base of the jacket and just over twice the depth of the waistband. Turn under all raw edges. Pin one long edge along the top of the waistband, fold the other long edge under to the inside of the jacket, and pin. Slipstitch in place (see page 121).

5. Separate the layers of petals from an imitation fabric flower. Using tiny running stitches (see page 120), stitch three flowers across the back of the jacket. Secure by stitching a button to the center of each flower.

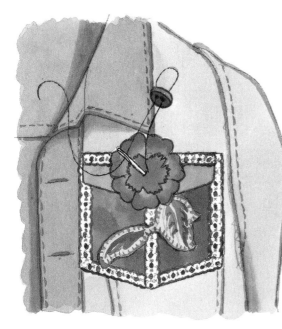

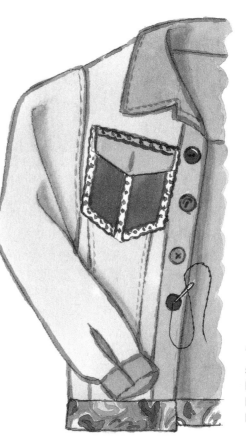

6. Select a flower and two leaves from the silk fabric and outline them in dimensional fabric paint. Leave to dry, then cut out. Using blanket stitch (see page 123), stitch one leaf on either side of the vertical strip of floral trim. Place the silk flower in the center of an imitation flower, with a small button on top, and then stitch to the left pocket flap, stitching through all layers.

7. Replace the studs on the button band with brightly colored buttons.

RIBBON CUFF
jacket

This is a good way of using up favorite strips of ribbon that are not long enough to go around the bottom of a skirt or down the legs of a pair of jeans. The orange and red base, and the bright colors and patterns of the ribbons, were inspired by the traditional colors of Mexican textiles and crafts, while the strips around the pockets remind me of military medals.

1. Alternating the colors, machine stitch pieces of red and orange woollen fabric or felt together to make a striped base. Pin, and then machine stitch strips of ribbon and fabric trim over the red-and-orange base.

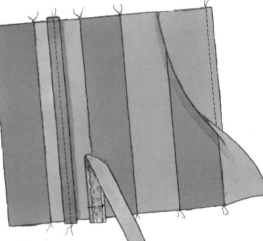

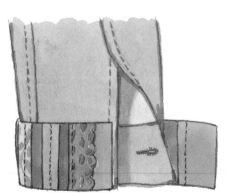

2. Using a pair of pliers, remove the metal studs from the jacket cuffs. Measure all around the cuffs, decide how deep you want the trim on the cuffs to be, and cut two pieces to this measurement.

3. Slipstitch (see page 121) a length of floral cotton trim to the top, bottom, and sides of each cuff trim. Slipstitch the trims to the cuffs, and attach snap fasteners. Make striped panels to go below the front right pocket and above the front left pocket in the same way.

IT'S ALL IN THE DETAIL

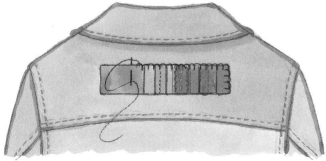

4. Cut another strip of striped fabric to go in the center of the back, and blanket stitch it in place (see page 123) to finish the design.

GLOVE
jacket

This is one of my favorite designs. I love the big roses: the one on the back of the jacket might just have been picked by the magical white kid glove, while the one on the front nods on its spindly, shiny stem amid a cloud of glittery sequins. I have really gone to town here: sometimes, going completely over the top is exactly the right thing to do!

you will need

Floral fabric
1 white kid glove
Green sequins
Green damask fabric
Shiny fabric
Blue/green PVC
Sequins in varying shapes and
    colors
Gold and silver glitter
    dimensional fabric paint
China floral buttons
Tailor's chalk or fabric marker
    pen
Needle
Embroidery threads
Sewing machine

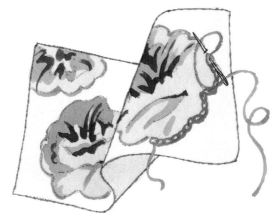

1. Select two large flowers from your chosen fabric and, using matching embroidery thread, chain stitch around the outline of each one (see page 123). Cut out, cutting as close to the stitching as possible.

2. Carefully pin and then machine stitch the kid glove to the lower part of the center back panel of the jacket, stitching as close to the edge of the glove as possible and leaving the thumb unstitched.

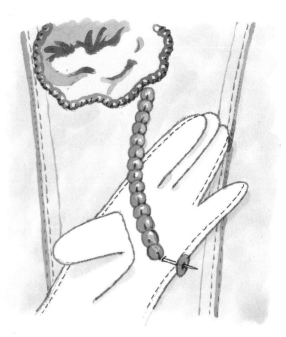

3. Pin one flower above the glove and, using matching thread, hand stitch it in place by working blanket stitch (see page 123) through the links of the chain stitch. Apply the other flower to the front left pocket in the same way.

4. Sew a wavy line of green sequins below the flowers to form the stems (see page 125). The stem on the back should go over the kid glove, while the stem on the front should extend to just above the waistband.

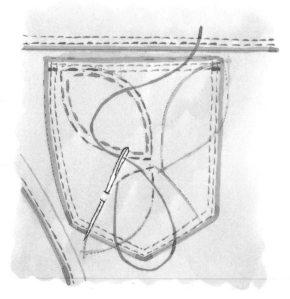

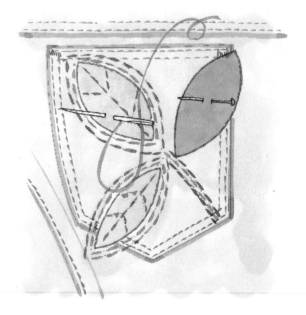

5. Using tailor's chalk or a fabric marker pen, draw leaf shapes coming out from the stems. Draw three more leaf shapes on the front right pocket. Work two rows of running stitch close together around two of the leaf outlines — one in blue thread and one in green.

6. Trace the leaf shapes onto damask, PVC, or shiny fabric and cut out. Pin the leaves in place inside the stitched outlines, and then form the veins by working a line of running stitch down the center of each leaf and out to the sides at a 45° angle. Edge the leaves on the front left pocket with gold glitter dimensional fabric paint, and leave to dry.

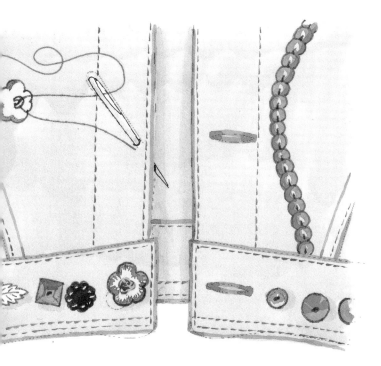

7. Fill in the remainder of the front left pocket with multi-colored sequins in varying sizes. Stitch a row of sequins along the waistband. Replace the existing buttons with floral ones.

8. Edge one of the leaves on the front right pocket with sequins, and fill in the background to the front right pocket with silver glitter dimensional fabric paint. Leave to dry.

SARI jacket

The beautiful gold embroidery on this sari fabric transforms this jacket from casual denim to a more structured and sophisticated-looking garment. The cropped, wide sleeve is elegant and the shape of the jacket is both feminine and glamorous, echoing the qualities of the sari fabric.

you will need

Embroidered sari fabric

Needle

Matching thread

1. Cut the bottom off the jacket just above the waistband, and cut off the lower part of the sleeves at the elbow. If necessary, use pliers to remove any metal studs that will be covered by the sari fabric border.

2. Cut a deep panel of sari fabric to go around the base of the jacket, turn under all raw edges, and press. Slipstitch to the base of the jacket (see page 121). Cut two rectangles of sari fabric to go above the pocket flaps, turn under all raw edges, and slipstitch in place.

3. For the sleeves, cut panels of sari fabric twice the depth that you want the cuffs to be and turn under all raw edges. Slipstitch the top of the cuffs to the base of the sleeves, then turn the sleeves inside out. Fold back the sari fabric to the right level, then slipstitch the edge to the base of the denim sleeves.

IT'S ALL IN THE DETAIL

TATTOO
jacket

A jacket for a boy — carefully hand stitched, but not in the least bit feminine. I have used classic tattoo motifs – a bluebird and a heart-and-arrow — which give the jacket a biker feel. The embroidery is done on pockets removed from old jeans, as it's much easier to stitch onto a small piece of fabric than to try and work embroidery over a tight-fitting sleeve.

you will need

Templates on page 127

Tracing paper and pencil

Tailor's chalk or fabric
   marker pen

3 back pockets cut from
   old jeans

Red satin fabric

Turquoise satin fabric

Needle

Sewing thread to match
   the denim

Embroidery threads: black,
   white, yellow

Small, sharp scissors

Sewing machine

1. Enlarge the heart-and-arrow template on page 127 to the required size, trace it onto one back pocket cut from a pair of old jeans, and, using black embroidery thread, chain stitch around the outline of the hearts and scrolls (see page 123).

2. Using a small, sharp pair of scissors and taking care not to cut through the stitching, cut out the interior of the hearts.

3. Place a piece of red satin fabric behind the cut-out hearts, and stitch it in place by working blanket stitch (see page 123) through the links of the chain stitch.

4. Using black embroidery thread, chain stitch the outline of the arrow. Using white embroidery thread, work a single line of running stitch (see page 120) around the inside of each of the scrolls. Using yellow thread, fill in the center of the arrow head and the feathers with randomly spaced running stitches.

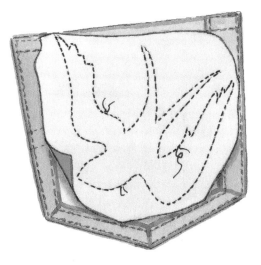

5. Enlarge the bluebird template on page 127 to the required size, trace it onto another back pocket cut from a pair of old jeans and, using black embroidery thread, chain stitch around the outline. Taking care not to cut through the stitching, cut out the interior of the bird.

6. Place a piece of blue satin fabric behind the cut-out bird shape, and pin it in place. Machine stitch around the outer edge of your hand-worked chain stitches.

You can use any motif you like for the "tattoos" but make sure it has a strong, clearly defined shape that is not too fiddly to cut around and that the fabric you place behind the cut-out shape provides a strong contrast in color to the denim of the jacket.

7. Slipstitch the decorated heart pocket to the left sleeve and the bird pocket to the right front of the jacket (see page 121). Slipstitch the undecorated pocket to the right sleeve.

POPPY POCKET
jacket

The bold wool poppy design gives this jacket a hand-worked quality, while the sumptuous, colorful fabrics give it a slight gypsy feel. A pretty diamanté button forms the center of the flower and holds together the bright scraps of fabric; it is also repeated at the buttonhole. The other pocket has a posy patch and some pretty buttons, which match those on the cuff.

you will need

Template on page 126

Tracing paper and pencil

Pink felted wool

Lilac felted wool

Needle and embroidery threads

1 large, plain button

3 diamanté buttons

Small piece of floral fabric

6 pink pearly buttons

4 green buttons

Tiny scraps of contrasting fabrics

1. Enlarge the template on page 126 to the required size (see page 118). Trace the outer and inner flowers onto felted wool, and cut out. Pin together, and chain stitch an oval petal shape through each inner petal (see page 123).

2. Place a large, plain button in the center of the flower, with a diamanté button on top, and sew them securely together.

3. Pin the flower to the jacket below the pocket and, using running stitch (see page 120) and matching embroidery thread, stitch it in place.

4. Cut floral fabric to fit the pocket flap and slipstitch in place (see page 121). Add two pink and two green buttons. Stitch scraps of contrasting fabrics and a diamanté button to the lapel. Sew a diamanté button to the jacket front, and one green and two pink buttons to each cuff.

PEARLY QUEEN
bag

This tiny bag, just big enough for a lipstick and keys, is a special little thing. I was given the vintage trim by a friend and it's beautiful: it must once have been part of a very elaborate and elegant dress, although who knows which decade — or even which century — it comes from. This scrap from the past, twinkling as it catches the light, really makes this bag precious.

Pale blue denim fabric
Vintage pearly sequin trim
Lining fabric in a contrasting color
Peach satin ribbon
Peach velvet ribbon
Lace
Pearl buttons and beads
Sewing machine
Matching sewing threads
Sewing needle

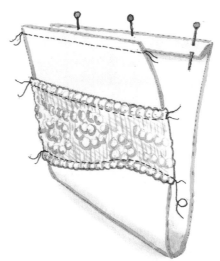

1. Cut a piece of pale blue denim fabric measuring roughly 14 x 8 in. (35 x 20 cm). Hand stitch the vintage trim near the top of one short end of the fabric. Turn under the short raw ends of the denim fabric and machine stitch.

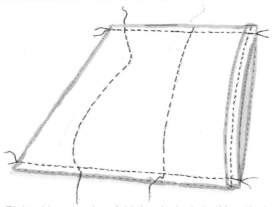

2. Right sides together, fold the denim in half lengthwise and machine stitch the sides, taking a ¼-in. (0.5-cm) seam. Press the seams open and turn right side out.

IT'S ALL IN THE DETAIL

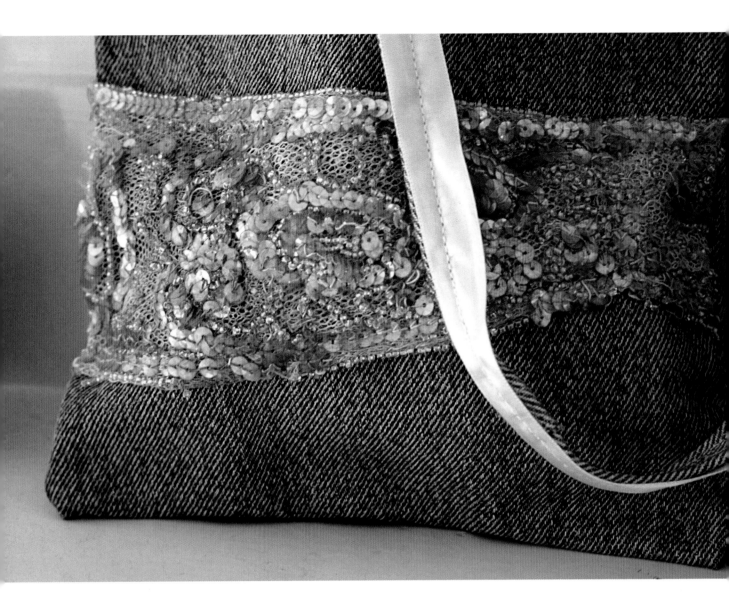

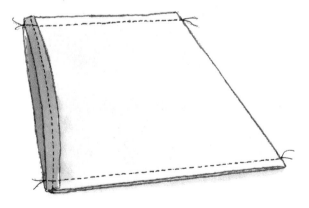

3. Repeat Steps 1 and 2 to make the lining, but do not turn the lining right side out at this stage.

4. To make the strap, cut a 22 x 1-in. (55 x 2.5-cm) strip of pale blue denim fabric. Place it right side down on your work surface, fold the long edges in to the center, and press. Machine stitch along each long edge. Center a strip of peach satin ribbon on the right side of the strap, and machine stitch along each long edge of the ribbon.

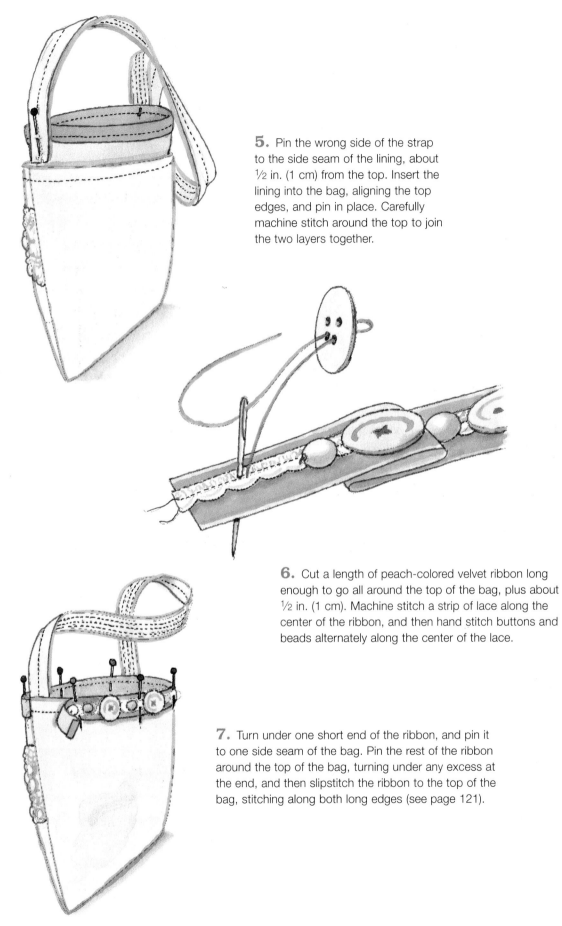

5. Pin the wrong side of the strap to the side seam of the lining, about ½ in. (1 cm) from the top. Insert the lining into the bag, aligning the top edges, and pin in place. Carefully machine stitch around the top to join the two layers together.

6. Cut a length of peach-colored velvet ribbon long enough to go all around the top of the bag, plus about ½ in. (1 cm). Machine stitch a strip of lace along the center of the ribbon, and then hand stitch buttons and beads alternately along the center of the lace.

7. Turn under one short end of the ribbon, and pin it to one side seam of the bag. Pin the rest of the ribbon around the top of the bag, turning under any excess at the end, and then slipstitch the ribbon to the top of the bag, stitching along both long edges (see page 121).

SPARKLE LEAF POCKET bag

This bag can be made from start to finish in about an hour. What I love about it is that almost everything has already been done for you: the pockets, strap side seams, and top hem are already there, leaving you more time to have fun decorating it.

you will need

1 pair of old jeans
Fabric marker pen
Gold lamé fabric
3 flower-shaped buttons
Floral fabric
Sewing machine
Sewing thread
Needle
Green embroidery thread
Small, sharp scissors

1. Cut a piece from the lower leg of a pair of old jeans, turn inside out, and machine stitch across the raw edge. Turn right side out.

2. To make the strap, remove the waistband from the jeans and slipstitch one end to each side of the top of the bag (see page 121), so that you have a buttonhole on one side and a stud on the other. (You could attach the waistband by machine, if you prefer.)

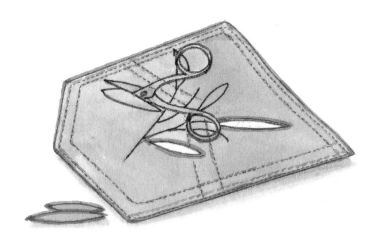

3. Cut the two back pockets off the old jeans. Referring to the photo opposite, draw leaves and stems freehand on one pocket. Using small, sharp scissors, cut out the interior of each leaf shape.

4. Place a square of gold lamé fabric behind the pocket and pin around the edges, keeping the lamé fabric taut. Using dark green thread, machine stitch around the leaves and up and down the stems several times, to define the stems clearly and make the stitching strong.

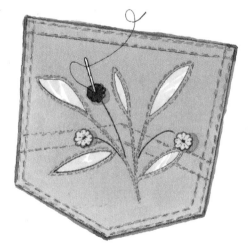

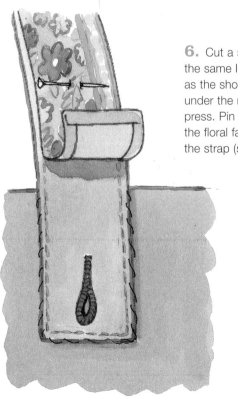

6. Cut a strip of floral fabric the same length and width as the shoulder strap. Turn under the raw edges and press. Pin and then slipstitch the floral fabric to the top of the strap (see page 121).

5. Sew three flower-shaped buttons in place on the pocket. Using green embroidery thread, work a neat line of chain stitch (see page 123) from each button down to one of the main machine-stitched stems.

7. Cut another strip of floral fabric for the other back pocket, which you cut off the jeans in Step 3. Turn under the raw edges and press. Pin and then slipstitch the floral fabric to the top of the pocket.

8. Slipstitch both pockets onto the front of the bag, overlapping them as shown.

PEARLY FLOWER
bag

I chose a dark denim — almost a midnight blue — for this design as I wanted to make a sophisticated-looking evening bag. The flowers and leaves are cut from a vintage lace crochet tablemat. The flower is edged with pretty sequins, while the flower center consists of a large pearl button topped with tiny pearl beads.

you will need

17½ x 8½-in. (44 x 21-cm)
  piece of dark denim
Sewing machine
Needle and embroidery threads
Lace crochet
1 large pearl button
3 small pearl beads
White sequins
Shiny trim
17½ x 8½-in. (44 x 21-cm)
  piece of fabric for lining
30 x 3½-in. (75 x 9-cm) piece
  of dark denim for strap

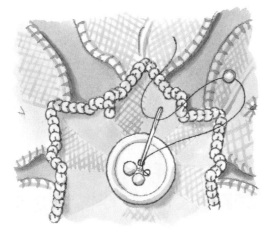

1. Turn under a ¼-in. (0.5-cm) double hem at each short end of the denim, and pin. Machine stitch along the short ends.

2. Cut out a flower and leaf motif from the lace crochet, and blanket stitch (see page 123) the motif to the top half of the denim. Place a large pearl button in the center of the flower and stitch in place, attaching three or four tiny pearl beads to the button center. Stitch white sequins around the edge of the flower (see page 125).

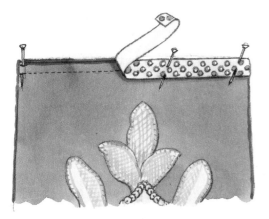

3. Fold the denim fabric in half, right sides together. Pin and then machine stitch the side seams, taking a ¼-in. (0.5-cm) seam. Turn right side out, then slipstitch a length of shiny trim around the top of the bag (see page 121).

4. Construct a bag from the lining fabric in the same way as you did with the denim, but do not turn right side out. Fold the denim fabric for the strap in half, right sides together. Machine stitch along the long raw edges, then turn right side out. Machine stitch the strap to the wrong side of the lining, centering it along the top edge. Place the lining inside the denim bag, pin in place, and blanket stitch (see page 123) around the top edge.

pearly flower bag ✽ 91

The sources of inspiration for these designs include flamenco dancers' dresses, ancient symbols, and even the heavens above! Gorgeous and girly, sexy and swirly, they're the very height of femininity and can be adapted for all ages.

skirts
AND
dresses

SUNSHINE skirt

For this skirt, I have created a patchwork from vibrant scraps of silk and cotton, with strong patterns and jewelike colors. I can imagine wearing it on a beach in the Mediterranean or California, where the colors would glow even more brightly in the strong summer sunshine.

you will need

- Selection of brightly colored fabric scraps
- Old tie
- Fabric scissors
- Sewing machine
- Needle and matching sewing thread

1. Cut strips of brightly colored fabric measuring roughly 6 x 3½ in. (15 x 9 cm). Right sides together, machine stitch one strip to the next down one short side. Repeat until the patchwork strip is long enough to go all around the base of the skirt and the tops of the back pockets, plus about 2 in. (5 cm) to allow for turning under the ends. Press open all seams.

2. Measure around the base of the skirt and cut the patchwork to this length plus about ¾ in. (2 cm). Turn under the long raw edges, and press. Machine stitch along one long edge; this will be the bottom edge of the skirt.

3. Pin the unmachined edge of the strip along the base of the skirt, turning under the short ends so that the ends of the strips align. Machine stitch in place.

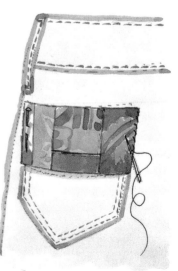

4. Cut the surplus patchwork into two pieces the same width as one of the back pockets plus about ½ in. (1.5 cm). Turn under the raw edges, and press. Slipstitch one section to the top of each pocket (see page 121). Thread an old tie through the belt loops, and tie at the front.

IT'S ALL IN THE DETAIL

GYPSY skirt

A pretty, gypsy-style skirt for all occasions, this design could be worn with boots, sandals, or even dancing shoes. The pink and pale green in the tie and ruffle are set off by the sparkly gold trim. With its tassels and frill, this skirt has a hint of the flamenco dancer's flamboyance — definitely an outfit to get your toes tapping!

you will need

Woven, tasselled scarf

Wide gold ribbon

Purple and yellow upholstery ribbon

2 belt loops cut from old jeans

Fabric scissors

Needle and basting thread

Sewing machine and matching sewing thread

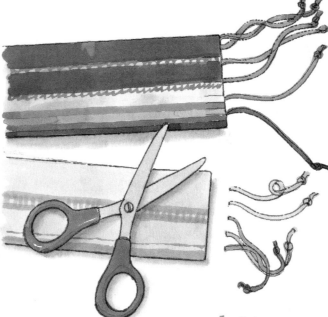

1. Cut your woven scarf in half lengthwise and remove the tassels from one piece.

2. Cut a piece of thread long enough to run the full length of the scarf. Sew a neat running stitch (see page 120) along one long edge of the piece of scarf from which you've removed the tassels. Pull the ends of the thread to gather the fabric lightly, making sure the ruffles are even. The ruffled strip should be the same length as the base of the skirt. Secure with a knot.

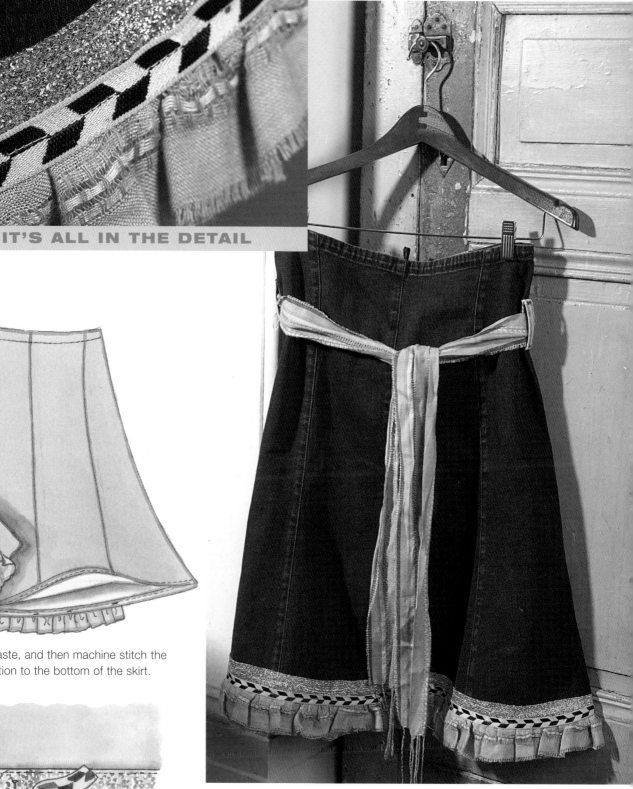

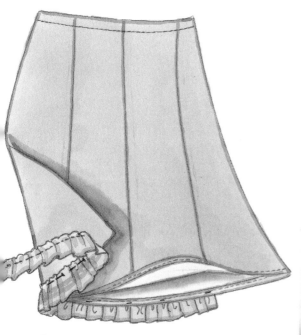

3. Pin, baste, and then machine stitch the ruffled section to the bottom of the skirt.

4. Machine stitch wide gold ribbon above the top edge of the ruffled section, with a thin strip of patterned upholstery ribbon on top, overlapping both the gold ribbon and the top of the ruffled section. Sew two belt loops cut from old jeans onto the hips of the skirt, and thread through the tasselled piece of scarf to use as a belt.

gypsy skirt ✳ **97**

BUTTERFLY
skirt

Template on page 127

Tracing paper and pencil

Fabric marker pen or tailor's chalk

Pale blue satin fabric

Green silk or satin fabric

Gold silk or satin fabric

Purple lace with a floral pattern

Voile with a butterfly motif

Butterfly buttons

Purple sequins

Needle and sewing threads

Embroidery threads

This skirt is a garden, with little floral patches on which the butterflies can alight. The embroidery on the large butterfly on the front of the skirt is both decorative and functional, as it holds the fabric in place while the bright stitching creates texture across the fabric.

1. Enlarge the template on page 127 to the required size (see page 118), trace onto pale blue satin fabric, cut out, and pin to the front of the skirt. Work a line of satin stitch (see page 122) down the center to attach the fabric to the skirt and form the butterfly's body. Alternating colors for each row, sew curving lines of running stitch (see page 120) over the wings, extending onto the denim.

2. Make four decorative patches for the back and front pockets. Cut a small piece of silk or satin fabric (gold for the front, green for the back) and sew a small piece of purple lace (for the plants) and a piece of voile with a butterfly motif onto each one.

3. Using neat running stitch or backstitch (see pages 120–121), stitch the patches in place.

4. Attach butterfly buttons to the front of the skirt, and sew purple sequins around the base of the front pockets (see page 125).

CUT-WORK MINI
skirt

Cut-work is usually used in the making of underwear, using fine silks and lace — but I think it can be more versatile than this. With the decoration here, I have layered fabrics together as well as cutting it away. The lace stands out against the dark denim and emphasizes the positives and the negatives — the sewing together and the cutting away.

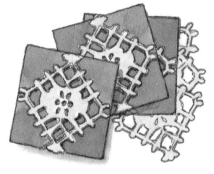

1. From your strip of lace crochet, cut out six diamond shapes approximately 2–3 in. (5–7 cm) square. Cut three squares of dark blue denim fabric the same size. Using blanket stitch (see page 123) and matching thread, sew three of the diamonds onto denim squares.

2. Using small, sharp scissors, cut away the denim fabric from behind the holes in two of the lace crochet pieces, leaving the linking strands intact. Space all three denim squares evenly along the base of the front of the skirt, leaving space for another square in between them, and stitch them in place using running stitch (see page 120).

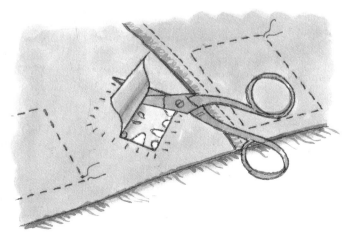

3. Pin the remaining lace diamonds in place between the denim squares. Using blanket stitch and matching thread, sew them in place. Using small, sharp scissors, cut away the skirt fabric behind the holes in the lace, leaving the linking strands intact.

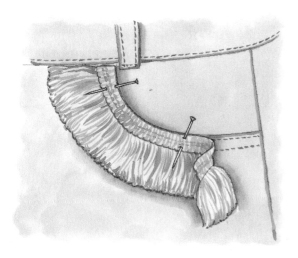

4. Blanket stitch a strip of lace along the top of each back pocket. Add a strip of fluffy blue upholstery trim above each one, and use the same trim to embellish the top of the pockets on the front of the skirt.

TREE OF LIFE
skirt

The Tree of Life, with its branches reaching up into the sky and its roots deep into the earth, is found in many cultures and represents a link between heaven, the earth, and the underworld.

Templates on page 126

Tracing paper and pencil

Marker pen or tailor's chalk

Burgundy-red satin fabric

Patterned silk fabric

Pink velvet fabric

Pink lace

Red glitter dimensional fabric
   paint

Red Chinese brocade

Flowery ribbon

Needle

Embroidery threads in colors
   of your choice

Small, sharp scissors

1. Enlarge the large tree of life template on page 126 to the required size, and trace it onto burgundy-red satin fabric (see page 119). Using different shades of green embroidery thread, chain stitch around the outline of each leaf (see page 123). Chain stitch along the stems.

2. Using small, sharp scissors, cut away the interior of the leaves. Place a small piece of fabric behind each leaf. I used patterned silk for two of the leaves and pink velvet for the others. Pin and baste in place (see page 120).

There is quite a lot of stitching involved in this skirt, but the curve and flow of the design make picking out the leaf shapes a satisfying task.

3. Stitch the fabric patches in place by working blanket stitch (see page 123) through the links of the chain stitch outline. I used a different color of thread on two of the leaves to give variety.

4. On the central pink velvet leaf, work three ovals in chain stitch. Using small, sharp scissors, cut away the center of the ovals. Place a tiny piece of pink lace behind each cut-out shape, and stitch in place by working blanket stitch through the links of the chain stitch.

5. Cut around the shape of the embroidery. Apply red glitter dimensional fabric paint to the edges to seal them. Using green embroidery thread and running stitch (see page 120), stitch the embroidery to the left front of the skirt, and then work blanket stitch all around the edge.

6. Trace the small leaf template on page 126 onto a separate piece of burgundy-red satin. Using green embroidery thread, chain stitch around the outline, and then work rows of neat running stitch for the veins. Cut out and apply to the right front of the skirt, as in Step 5, but this time use red embroidery thread.

7. Cut a square of red Chinese brocade, and slipstitch narrow flowery ribbon around all four edges (see page 121). Blanket stitch the square under the right front pocket flap.

RIBBONS AND BOW
skirt

I think of this skirt as being very girly and a little bit flirtatious — 'sugar and spice and all things nice,' as the nursery rhyme goes. The feminine-looking lace, silk, and soft velvet ribbon contrast with the shiny PVC, while the strong colors and varied textures create a bold yet balanced design.

Pink lace

Green satin ribbon

Floral ribbon

Pale blue velvet ribbon

Tracing paper and pencil

Pink PVC

Sewing machine

Sewing threads

1. Cut a triangle of pink lace. Machine stitch it to the center front of the skirt, below the zipper.

2. Cut a length of green satin ribbon and a length of floral ribbon long enough to cover the two long sides of the lace triangle, plus about 2 in. (5 cm). Machine stitch the floral ribbon to the center of the green satin ribbon.

3. Pin, and then machine stitch the green ribbon over the long edges of the lace triangle. You will need to fold the ribbon over and then back on itself, as shown, to form a neat apex at the top of the triangle.

IT'S ALL IN THE DETAIL

4. Tie a piece of green satin ribbon in a bow, and secure it in the center with a tiny stitch. Hand stitch the bow to the top of the triangle.

5. Cut a length of floral ribbon twice the height of one back pocket plus about 4 in. (10 cm) and a length of pale blue velvet ribbon the same size. Machine stitch the floral ribbon to the center of the velvet ribbon, then cut two lengths the height of the pocket plus about ½ in. (1 cm), reserving the rest for the belt loops.

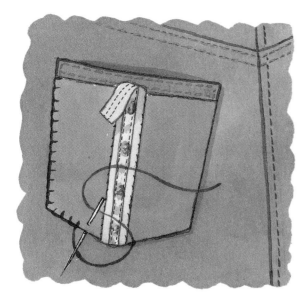

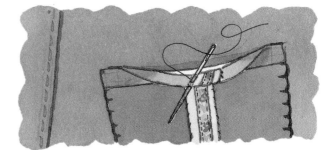

6. Trace around one of the back pockets to make a paper pattern. Place the pattern on pink PVC, and cut out two pockets. Slipstitch one length of velvet-and-floral ribbon vertically down the center of each pocket (see page 121). Using blanket stitch (see page 123) and matching thread, stitch the PVC patches on top of the back pockets, leaving the top edges open.

7. Turn the excess ribbon over to the inside of the denim pocket and slipstitch it in place.

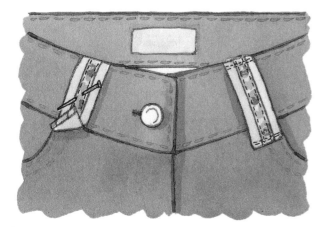

8. Remove the belt loops from the skirt. From the piece reserved in Step 5, cut two lengths of velvet-and-flowered ribbon the same size as the belt loops, remembering to allow an extra ½ in. (1 cm) or so on each piece for turning under the ends. Machine stitch the belt loops in place.

The shiny PVC pockets give this design a thoroughly contemporary feel that contrasts boldly with the pretty pink lace, soft velvet, and floral ribbon.

HEAVENLY skirt

This design is about stimulating a child's imagination through touch, as well as through visual effects, so I have used tactile fabrics such as soft cashmere and gold leather, as well as buttons, beads, and sequins. Little fingers will love tracing their way across the night sky to catch a falling star!

1. For the "planets," cut six small circles from cashmere and leather. Pin them in place on the skirt, then stitch them in place using running or chain stitch (see pages 120 and 123).

2. Stitch on three button "moons" and four sequin stars, spacing them randomly.

3. Stitch a bead or a sequin to the center of each star (see page 125).

SWEETHEART
babydress

This is the perfect dress to take your first steps in — what little girl would not adore it? The twinkling green cat arches her back as she slinks past the bright patch pocket. The heart motif on the front is cheerful, bright, and picked out in tiny red beads.

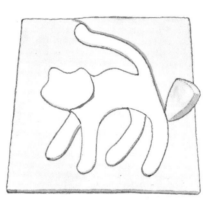

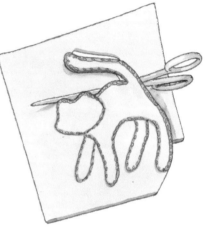

1. Enlarge the cat template on page 127 to the required size and, using tailor's chalk, draw around it on green felted wool. Chain stitch around the drawn outline (see page 123).

2. Carefully cut out the motif, cutting as close to the stitching as possible.

Every little girl loves a bit of glitz and glitter, so the simple appliqué motifs on this dress, embellished with sequins and tiny beads, are surefire winners!

IT'S ALL IN THE DETAIL

3. Draw in the cat's features and sew over them, using chain stitch for the mouth and two small running stitches (see page 120) for the eyes. Sew sequins across the cat's body and down her tail (see page 125).

4. Cut a 4-in. (10-cm) square of pink felted wool. Turn under the raw edges of the shiny fabric, and press. Place the shiny fabric along the top of the pink felted wool square, wrapping the short ends around the edges, and machine stitch.

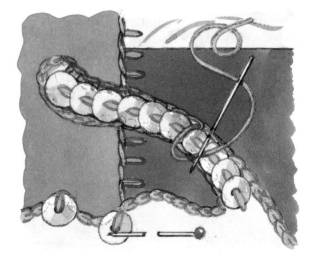

5. Pin, then machine stitch the pocket to the dress, then blanket stitch around the sides and bottom edge (see page 123).

6. Pin the cat over the edge of the pocket, then stitch it in place by working blanket stitch through the links of the chain stitch.

Appliqué motifs are a simple way of decorating plain-coloured denim — and if you cut them from felt or blanket fabric, as here, they won't fray so you don't need to worry about turning under the edges.

7. Enlarge the heart template on page 127 and cut two small hearts from pink felted wool. Pin one to the front pocket, and stitch it in place using running stitch, attaching a tiny red bead with every stitch.

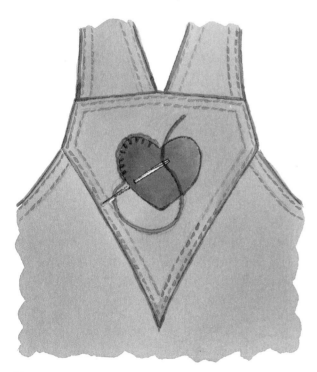

8. Pin the second heart to the back of the dress, and blanket stitch it in place, using a contrasting color of thread.

TULIP apron

This pretty denim apron would make a lovely gift for Mother's Day. The little denim pocket forms a plant pot, while the heavy tulip flowers loll and shimmer above it. The stitching is bold and the design clean and simple — and is there any reason not to wear sequins in the kitchen?!

you will need

One back pocket cut from old jeans

Seam ripper

Narrow green ribbon

Templates on page 127

Tracing paper and pencil

Tailor's chalk or marker pencil

Green woollen fabric or felt

Green sequins

Pink velvet fabric

Needle

Embroidery threads

1. Using a seam ripper, remove a back pocket from an old pair of jeans. Place it on the front of the apron, slightly off center, and slipstitch it in place (see page 121). Cut two lengths of narrow green ribbon and, using matching thread and tiny running stitches (see page 120), stitch them to the apron, coming out of the top of the pocket, bending one of the lengths at an angle, as shown.

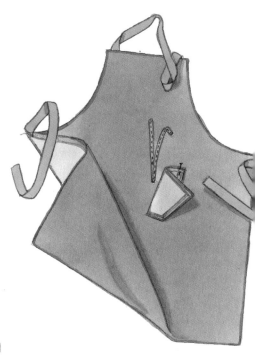

2. Enlarge the template on page 127 to the required size, trace the leaf shapes onto green woollen fabric or felt, and cut out. Using running stitch and matching thread, sew them to the apron. One leaf should come out of the top of the pocket, and the other should flop down over the pocket. Sew a row of sequins down the center of each leaf (see page 125).

3. Trace the enlarged tulip flower shapes onto pink velvet fabric. Chain stitch (see page 123) around the petals, using dark pink thread for the overall outline and front petals and a red for the back petals. Following the outline of the flower, work rows of running stitch (see page 120) around both tulips.

4. Cut out the tulip flowers, cutting as close to the chain stitch as possible. Position them at the top of the green ribbon stems, and stitch in place by working blanket stitch (see page 123) through the links of the chain stitch.

IT'S ALL IN THE DETAIL

TECHNIQUES

The techniques used in this book are all very simple and will allow you to customize and personalize your denim clothing quickly and easily.

USING TEMPLATES AND PATTERNS

Several of the projects in this book require you either to make a template that you can draw around to cut out a fabric shape or to trace and transfer an embroidery pattern onto your fabric.

ENLARGING MOTIFS TO THE REQUIRED SIZE

Although many books and patterns give motifs at actual size, it is useful to know how to enlarge them.

1. First, decide how big you want the motif to be on the finished garment. Let's say, for example, that you want a particular shape to be 4 in. (10 cm) tall.

2. Then measure the template that you are working from. Let's imagine that the template is smaller than the size you require — say, 2 in. (5 cm) tall.

3. Take the size that you want the motif to be (4 in./10 cm) and divide it by the actual size of the template (2 in./5 cm). Multiply that figure by 100 and you get 200 — so you need to enlarge the motif on a photocopier to 200%.

REDUCING MOTIFS TO THE REQUIRED SIZE

If you want a motif on the finished garment to be smaller than the template, the process is exactly the same. For example, if the template is 2 in. (5 cm) tall and you want the motif to be 1 in. (2.5 cm) tall, divide 1 in. (2.5 cm) by the actual size of the template (2 in./5 cm) and multiply by 100, which gives you a figure of 50. So the figure that you need to key in on the photocopier is 50%.

MAKING A TEMPLATE

To make a template for a shape that you want to appliqué onto another piece of fabric, such as the cat on page 112, first enlarge (or reduce) the motif to the size you want.

1. Using a thick black pencil, trace the motif onto tracing paper.

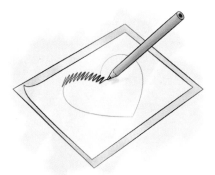

2. Turn the tracing paper over, place it on card, and scribble over your drawn lines to transfer them to the card.

3. Finally, cut out the card shape using scissors or a craft knife on a cutting mat. You can now place the card template on your chosen fabric and draw around it with tailor's chalk or a fabric marker pen to transfer the shape to the fabric.

TRANSFERRING EMBROIDERY PATTERNS ONTO FABRIC

First enlarge (or reduce) the motif to the size you want. Then, using a soft, black pencil, trace the motif onto tracing paper.

If your fabric is light colored and light in weight (cotton, for example), you can tape the tracing paper to a light box, with the fabric right side up on top. (If you do not have a light box, tape the tracing paper and fabric to a window.) You should be able to see the pattern through the fabric. Now go over the lines again, using tailor's chalk or a fabric marker pen. (You can buy special fadeaway marker pens, which means that you do not have to worry about the drawn lines being visible on the fabric after the embroidery is completed. The drawback of these, however, is that the lines fade within a few days, so you can't transfer the pattern and then put everything away in a drawer for a few weeks — otherwise you'll be back to square one!)

If your fabric is dark colored or very heavy (denim, for example), your best option is to use light-colored dressmaker's carbon paper. Simply photocopy or trace your pattern onto normal paper, and then place the fabric right side up on your work surface, with the carbon paper on top (carbon side down), and go over the outline. You can use the carbon-paper method for light-colored fabrics, too — and here, normal graphite or blue carbon paper will work well. You should be able to wash out the lines once you have completed the embroidery.

STITCHES

There are literally hundreds of different stitches. Some are designed to be virtually invisible, while others are used purely for decorative effect. Here are some of the most common and useful, ranging from "joining" stitches for stitching two pieces of fabric together to edging stitches such as blanket stitch and "filling" stitches such as satin.

BASTING STITCH

Basting stitch is used to temporarily hold pieces of fabric in place until they have been sewn together permanently. Basting stitches are removed once the permanent stitching is complete. Use a contrasting color of thread, so that you can see it easily.

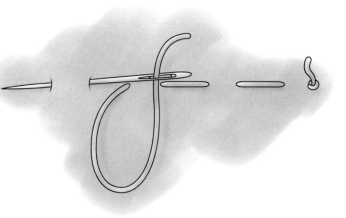

Knot the thread, and work a long running stitch through all layers of fabric.

RUNNING STITCH

Running stitch is probably the simplest hand stitch of all.

Work from right to left.

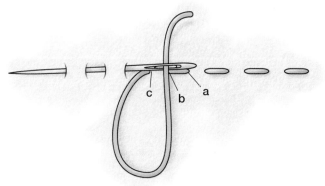

Bring the needle up at (a) on the front of the fabric. Take it down again at (b), and up again at (c). Repeat as required.

BACKSTITCH

Backstitch provides a continuous line of stitching. It can be used to join two pieces of fabric firmly together, and also for decorative effect.

Work from right to left.

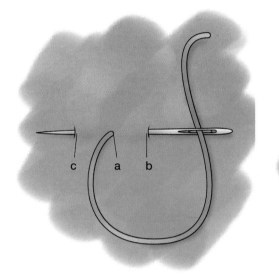 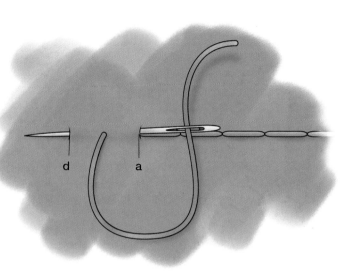

1. Bring the needle up at (a), on the front of the fabric. Take it down again at (b), a little to the right of where it first emerged, and up again at (c), a little to the left of where it first emerged. Make sure the distances between each point are the same.

2. To make the second stitch, take the needle down at (a), and bring it back up again at (d). Repeat as required.

SLIPSTITCH

This stitch is almost invisible and is an easy way of appliquéing one piece of fabric to another.

Work from right to left.

Slide the needle between the two pieces of fabric, bringing it out on the edge of the top fabric so that the knot in the thread is hidden between the two layers. Pick up one or two threads from the base fabric, then bring the needle up a short distance along, on the edge of the top fabric, and pull through. Repeat as required.

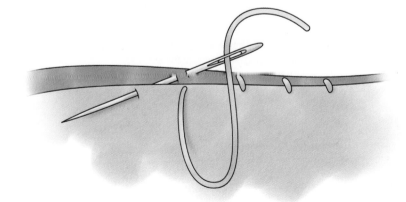

STEM STITCH

Not surprisingly, given the name, this stitch is often used to embroider flower stems. It can be worked in either straight or curved lines. Each stitch begins halfway along the previous stitch.

Work from left to right.

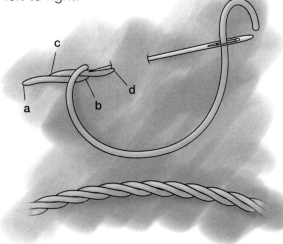

Bring the needle up at (a), and down at (b). Bring it up again at (c), halfway between (a) and (b), above the thread, and take it down again at (d).

SATIN STITCH

Satin stitch is used to "fill in" areas such as leaves and flower petals. Work the stitches very close together, so that no fabric shows in between them.

Work from left to right.

Bring the needle up at (a), and down at (b). Bring it up again at (c), making sure there is no gap between (a) and (c), and down again at (d). Repeat as required.

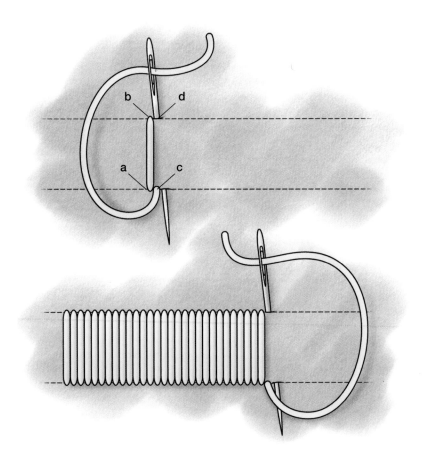

BLANKET STITCH

Blanket stitch was originally used to edge woollen blankets and prevent them from fraying — hence the name.

Work from left to right.

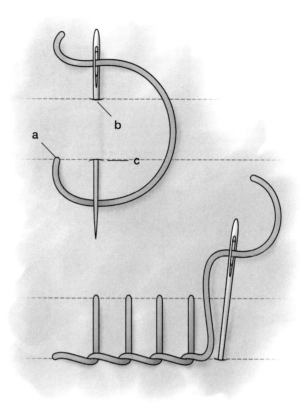

Bring the needle up at (a), down at (b), and up again at (c), looping the thread under the needle.

NOTE: If you are working this stitch along a raw edge, take the needle through the fabric only at point (b); bring it up again into "thin air" below the raw edge, so that the twisted edge of the stitch forms along the raw edge of the fabric.

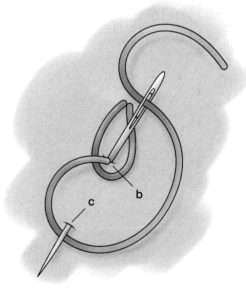

CHAIN STITCH

Chain stitch can be worked in straight or curved lines, and is a particularly effective way of embroidering flower and leaf stems and outlining motifs.

Work from right to left.

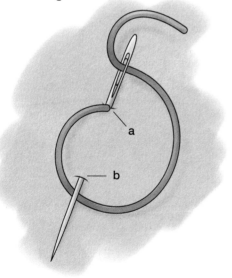

1. Bring the needle up at (a) and re-insert it in the same place, looping the thread below the needle. Bring the needle up at (b).

2. Re-insert the needle at (b), inside the loop formed by the first stitch. Bring the needle up at (c). Repeat as required.

CROSS STITCH

Cross stitch is often worked on a canvas fabric such as aida, where you can count the number of threads to make sure that the stitch lengths and distances are consistent. If you are working cross stitch on denim or a similar fabric, remember to keep both "arms" of the crosses exactly the same length.

Working a single cross stitch

Individual cross stitches, worked randomly across a piece of fabric, are a quick-and-easy way of adding color and interest. Depending on the thread color, they can look like tiny flowers, stars, or snowflakes.

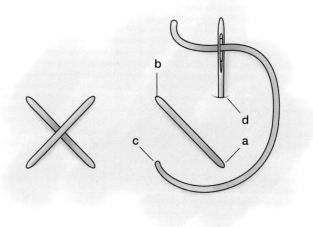

Bring the needle up at (a), down at (b), up at (c), and down at (d).

Working a line of cross stitch

A line (or several lines) of cross stitch is often worked to fill in an area. It can also used to outline a motif.

Work from right to left.

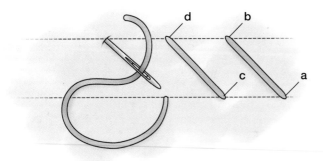

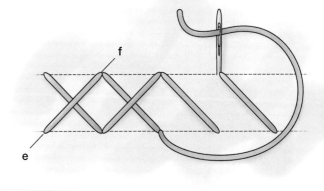

1. Bring the needle up at (a), down at (b), up at (c), down at (d), and so on, until you have reached the left-hand end of the line.

2. Bring the needle up at (e) and down at (f), across the first stitch in the line, to complete the cross shape. Repeat until you have reached the right-hand end of the line.

EMBELLISHMENTS

There is a vast array of embellishments to use on clothing, from buttons and beads to decorative trims.

STITCHING ON SEQUINS

The stitching is visible, so you need to decide whether to use matching thread or a contrasting thread, to make the stitching a decorative feature in its own right.

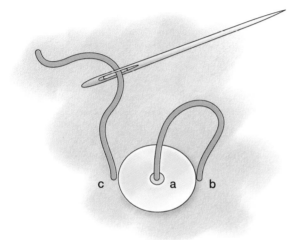

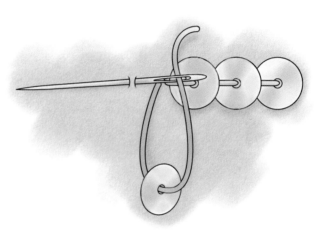

Bring the needle up through the fabric at (a), and thread on the first sequin. Take the needle down at (b), just over the right edge of the sequin. Bring the needle up at (c).

To attach a whole row of sequins, repeat to the left as required. The distance between (a) and (c) should be the width of one sequin, so that the sequins are just touching.

TEMPLATES

Enlarge these templates to the size you require, following the instructions on page 118.

baby face jeans
page 10

tree of life skirt
page 102

poppy pocket jacket
page 80

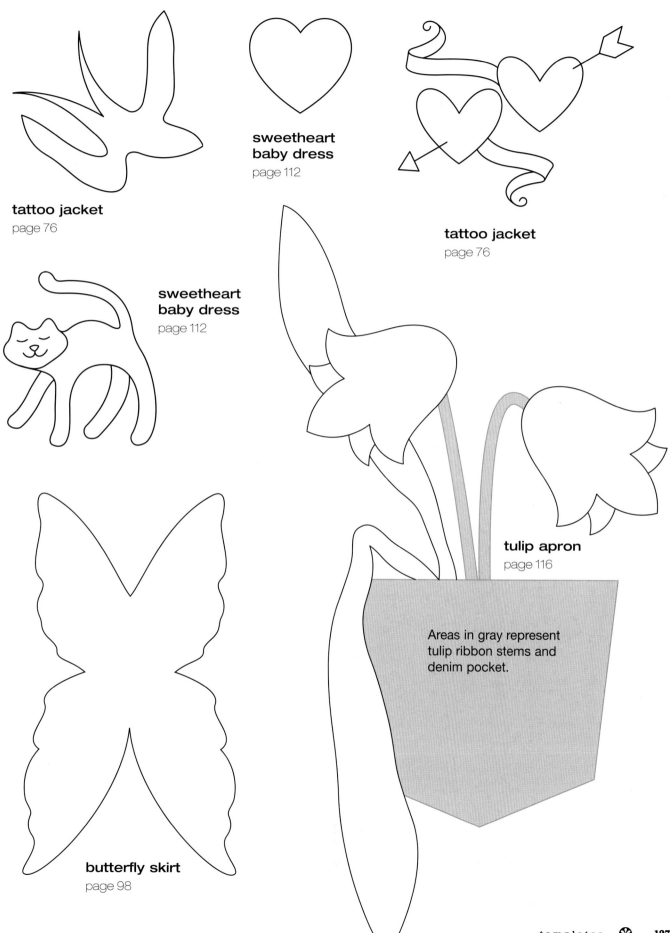

tattoo jacket
page 76

sweetheart baby dress
page 112

tattoo jacket
page 76

sweetheart baby dress
page 112

tulip apron
page 116

Areas in gray represent tulip ribbon stems and denim pocket.

butterfly skirt
page 98

INDEX